O Shenandoah

and other songs from the New World

arranged for violin and piano

Polly Waterfield

and

Louise Beach

FABER *ff* MUSIC

Foreword

Coming from both sides of the Atlantic, we have found ourselves drawn to traditional tunes from a wide range of origins; from Canadian to Celtic-influenced to the quintessentially American. We looked for songs with a certain quality of heart and eloquence, and aimed to turn them into 'simple gifts' for the elementary violinist. The original tunes are simple, but we have sought to place them on a large imaginative canvas and to enhance their innate elegance. If the collection opens up some musical horizons for students then we will have succeeded.

The collection is designed to be useful to the teacher looking for progressive repertoire from Grades 1–3: the keys have been specially chosen to cover most of the scales across those levels, and there is scope for position work. There are also opportunities for exploring harmonics, different kinds of pizzicato, col legno, and vibrato. All the pieces in this book are compatible with *O Shenandoah!* for viola and for cello, so they can also be used with mixed groups. We hope both young and old will enjoy the vibrancy and spaciousness of these songs.

Polly Waterfield
and
Louise Beach

© 2003 by Faber Muisic Ltd
First published in 2003 by Faber Music Ltd
3 Queen Square London WC1N 3AU
Cover illustration by Lynette Williamson
Cover design by Shireen Nathoo Design
Music processed by MusicSet 2000
Printed in England by Caligraving Ltd

ISBN 0-571-52224-6

To buy Faber Music publications or to find out about the full range of titles available please contact your local music retailer or Faber Music sales enquiries:

Faber Music Limited, Burnt Mill, Elizabeth Way, Harlow, CM20 2HX England
Tel: +44 (0)1279 82 89 82   Fax: +44 (0)1279 82 89 83
sales@fabermusic.com   fabermusic.com

CONTENTS

LAND OF THE SILVER BIRCH

This Canadian song needs a broad, singing style with plenty of bow. Try singing it to the words:

Land of the silver birch, home of the beaver, / Where still the mighty moose wanders at will. /
Blue lake and rocky shore, I will return once more, / Hi-ya-ya, hi-ya, Hi-ya-ya, hi-ya,
Hi-ya-ya, hi-ya, Ah …

LAND OF THE SILVER BIRCH

This Canadian song needs a broad, singing style with plenty of bow. Try singing it to the words:

Land of the silver birch, home of the beaver, / Where still the mighty moose wanders at will. /
Blue lake and rocky shore, I will return once more, / Hi-ya-ya, hi-ya, Hi-ya-ya, hi-ya,
Hi-ya-ya, hi-ya, Ah …

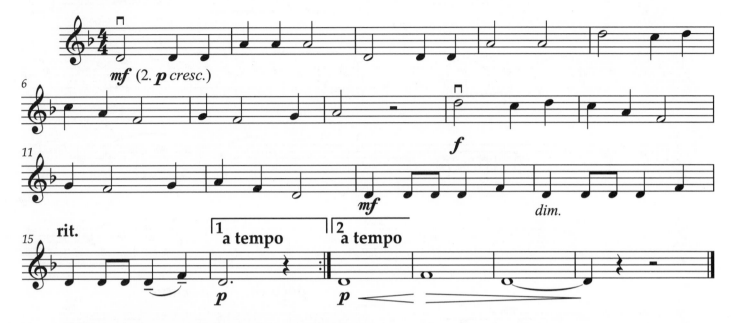

THE RAILROAD CORRAL

The 'chuckwagon' provided breakfast for the 'night riders' – cowboys who have been watching
the cattle at night. 'Flapjacks' are pancakes.

We're up in the morning ere breaking of day, / The chuckwagon's busy, the flapjack's in play, /
The herd is astir over hillside and vale, / With the night riders crowding them into the trail.

SIMPLE GIFTS

This Shaker hymn tune is known as 'The Lord of the Dance' in England.
The American composer Aaron Copland used it in his ballet 'Appalachian Spring'.

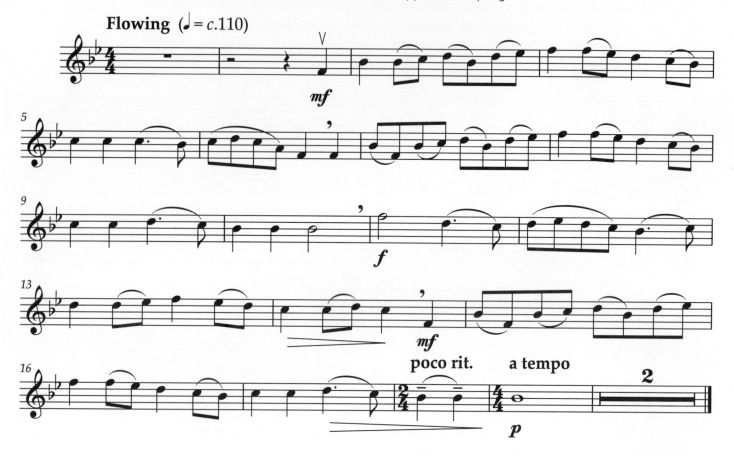

GROUNDHOG

In the Kentucky mountains they would hunt and roast the groundhog at the beginning
of spring, and eat it with relish!
Play this song with gusto, and call out 'Groundhog!' while you play.

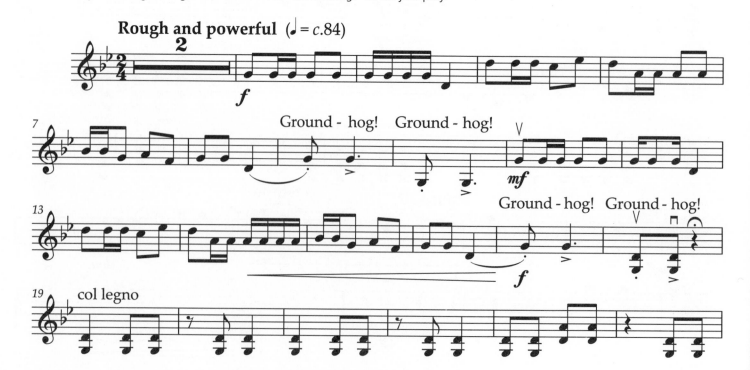

HI! SAYS THE BLACKBIRD

This whimsical song from New England tells why the blackbird is black, the woodpecker's head is red, and why the bat flies at night. Enjoy the conversation with the piano in the middle verse.

Hi! says the blackbird sitting on a chair, / Once I courted a lady fair, / She proved fickle and turned her back, / And ever since then I've dressed in black.

WONDROUS LOVE

This beautiful hymn tune is an opportunity to sing through your violin, enjoying the rise and
fall of the melody and, in the Variation, the interplay with the piano. If you do vibrato, use it!
The piece is complete at bar 21, but can also be played in an extended version by skipping the
1st and 2nd time bars, and continuing to the 3rd time bar, which leads into the Variation.

CAPE COD SHANTY

This piece can be easily played in 2nd position up to the pause in bar 32.

Cape Cod girls they have no combs, Heave away, heave away! / They comb their hair
with codfish bones, we are bound for Australia! / Cape Cod boys they have no sleds, /
They slide downhill on cod-fish heads, Heave away, heave away!

ALL THE PRETTY LITTLE HORSES

In this arrangement of a well-known lullaby the violin and piano take turns with the tune.

Hush-you-bye, don't you cry, go to sleepy, little baby. / When you wake, you shall have all
the pretty little horses. / Blacks and bays, dapples and grays, coach and six a-little horses. /
Hush-you-bye, don't you cry, go to sleepy, little baby.

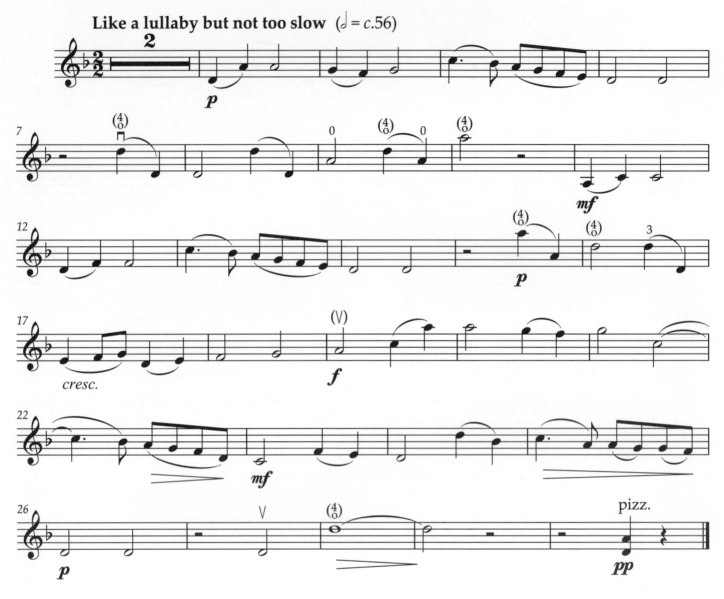

LADY ISABEL AND THE ELF KNIGHT

You can imagine your own story from the colourful title of this song, which is from Nova Scotia.
It needs to be played with a gentle lilt.

O SHENANDOAH!

This great song tells of a white trader who falls in love with an Indian girl. If you didn't grow up with the song you need to hear it a lot and sing it a lot, till you can conjure up in your playing the rolling river and the feeling of longing for something you love.

O Shenandoah, I love your daughter, / Away you rolling river, / For her I've crossed the rolling water, / Away we're bound away, / 'Cross the wide Missouri.

OLD JOE CLARK

There are hundreds of stories about Old Joe Clark, but nobody is sure who he was!
This is one of the most popular American songs.

Old Joe Clark he had a house, / Forty storeys high, / And every storey in that house
was lined with chicken pie. / Fare you well, old Joe Clark, / Fare you well I say,
Fare you well, old Joe Clark, / For I'm a-goin' away.

THE RAILROAD CORRAL

The 'chuckwagon' provided breakfast for the 'night riders' – cowboys who have been watching the cattle at night. 'Flapjacks' are pancakes.

We're up in the morning ere breaking of day, / The chuckwagon's busy, the flapjack's in play, / The herd is astir over hillside and vale, / With the night riders crowding them into the trail.

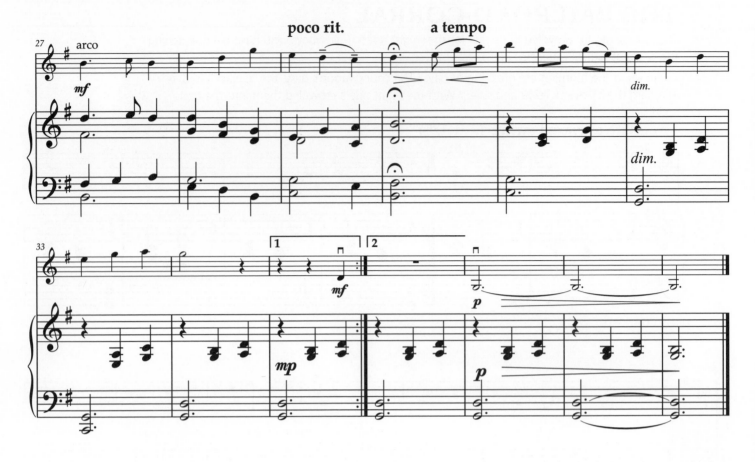

SIMPLE GIFTS

This Shaker hymn tune is known as 'The Lord of the Dance' in England.
The American composer Aaron Copland used it in his ballet 'Appalachian Spring'.

poco rit.   a tempo

GROUNDHOG

In the Kentucky mountains they would hunt and roast the groundhog at the beginning
of spring, and eat it with relish!
Play this song with gusto, and call out 'Groundhog!' while you play.

HI! SAYS THE BLACKBIRD

This whimsical song from New England tells why the blackbird is black, the woodpecker's head is red, and why the bat flies at night. Enjoy the conversation with the piano in the middle verse.

Hi! says the blackbird sitting on a chair, / Once I courted a lady fair, / She proved fickle and turned her back, / And ever since then I've dressed in black.

WONDROUS LOVE

This beautiful hymn tune is an opportunity to sing through your violin, enjoying the rise and
fall of the melody and, in the Variation, the interplay with the piano. If you do vibrato, use it!
The piece is complete at bar 21, but can also be played in an extended version by skipping the
1st and 2nd time bars, and continuing to the 3rd time bar, which leads into the Variation.

Variation
more freely, with warmth

CAPE COD SHANTY

This piece can be easily played in 2nd position up to the pause in bar 32.

Cape Cod girls they have no combs, Heave away, heave away! / They comb their hair
with codfish bones, we are bound for Australia! / Cape Cod boys they have no sleds, /
They slide downhill on cod-fish heads, Heave away, heave away!

ALL THE PRETTY LITTLE HORSES

In this arrangement of a well-known lullaby the violin and piano take turns with the tune.

Hush-you-bye, don't you cry, go to sleepy, little baby. / When you wake, you shall have all the pretty little horses. / Blacks and bays, dapples and grays, coach and six a-little horses. / Hush-you-bye, don't you cry, go to sleepy, little baby.

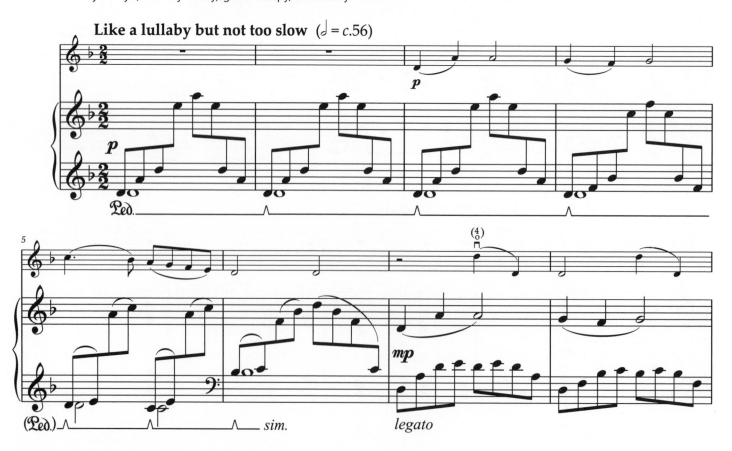

LADY ISABEL AND THE ELF KNIGHT

You can imagine your own story from the colourful title of this song, which is from Nova Scotia.
It needs to be played with a gentle lilt.

O SHENANDOAH!

This great song tells of a white trader who falls in love with an Indian girl. If you didn't grow up with the song you need to hear it a lot and sing it a lot, till you can conjure up in your playing the rolling river and the feeling of longing for something you love.

O Shenandoah, I love your daughter, / Away you rolling river, / For her I've crossed the rolling water, / Away we're bound away, / 'Cross the wide Missouri.

OLD JOE CLARK

There are hundreds of stories about Old Joe Clark, but nobody is sure who he was!
This is one of the most popular American songs.

Old Joe Clark he had a house, / Forty storeys high, / And every storey in that house
was lined with chicken pie. / Fare you well, old Joe Clark, / Fare you well I say,
Fare you well, old Joe Clark, / For I'm a-goin' away.

Variation I

Variation II

VIOLIN MUSIC FOR THE ESTABLISHED BEGINNER
FROM FABER MUSIC

The Young Violinist's Early Music Collection

10 gems for violin and piano
arranged by Edward Huws Jones

ISBN 0-571-51669-6

Up-Grade!

Light relief between grades
Pam Wedgwood

GRADES 1–2 ISBN 0-571-51954-7
GRADES 2–3 ISBN 0-571-51955-5

Position Pieces

Easy repertoire for violin and piano
in 2nd, 3rd and 4th positions
edited by Marguerite Wilkinson
and Alan Gout

ISBN 0-571-51436-7

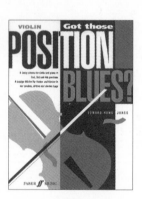

Got those Position Blues?

9 Jazzy pieces for violin and piano
in 2nd, 3rd and 4th positions
Edward Huws Jones

ISBN 0-571-51534-7

Gypsy Jazz

Songs and Dances from across
Europe for violin and piano
Polly Waterfield
and Timothy Kraemer

EASY LEVEL ISBN 0-571-51637-8
INTERMEDIATE LEVEL ISBN 0-571-51937-7

Jazzin' About

Fun pieces
for violin and piano
Pam Wedgwood

ISBN 0-571-51315-8

FABER ff MUSIC